Andrei Codrescu

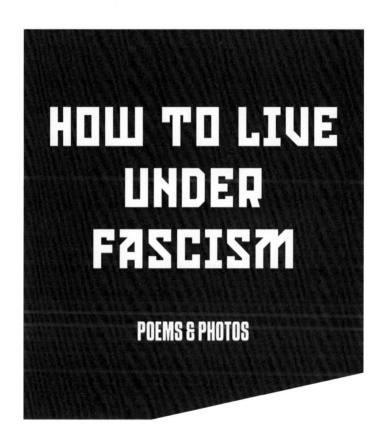

HOW TO LIVE UNDER FASCISM

POEMS & PHOTOS

BLACK
WIDOW
PRESS

BOSTON

Black Widow Press is an imprint of Commonwealth Books, Inc., Boston, MA. Distributed to the trade by Simon & Schuster throughout North America, Canada, and the U.K. Black Widow Press and its logo are registered trademarks of Commonwealth Books, Inc.

Joseph S. Phillips and Susan J. Wood, Ph.D., Publishers
www.blackwidowpress.com

Cover design & interior text production: Geoff Munsterman

ISBN-13: 979-8-9911391-5-1 (paperback)

Printed in the United States of America

TABLE OF CONTENTS

Note on *How to Live Under Fascism: Poems & Photos*

My new collection of poetry is a guide to living in the dictatorship of the new American plutocracy. I was born and raised in Romania, a national-socialist client of the Soviet empire, where poetry was always a nightmare for the state, and a lifeline to the terrified citizen. I emigrated to freedom in the U.S., where the subversive powers of poetry were slowly dissolving into badly-payed entertainment for easily distracted readers. The surveillance of the market wasn't yet as deadly as that of the communist censors, but their merger seems a done deal now. In the face of this civic catastrophy poetry has to be more than eau-de-cologne to dispel the stink of army boots. This book is occasionally clear about that, but there are also poems of love and the plague, childhood scents, the warmth of other bodies, the warnings of history, and the pleasure of making things up. I was taking photographs on my daily walks when writing these poems, without meaning to use them, but then I saw that they were strangely and not so strangely connected. My mother and father were photographers in the bad old days, I think their craft shadowed me. I dedicate these works to them.

HOW TO LIVE UNDER FASCISM

zoom caviar onegin

when we met for the first time in park slope
our board had zoom caviar

we crunched fish eggs served by ballerinas
who defected from russia on pointe

we drank zoom champagne from their slippers
until they turned into steel black combat boots
pointed at putin's crotch

the sweat of our attention
increased drop by drop like a fetus outgrowing its jar

art said a tight-lipped goodbye to classical grandeur
leaving millions of dollars in baby mink fur hats

in russia the masses eat the gunpowder of grenades
mixed with bolshoi sawdust and swan lake algae slime

news

you're the swan in swan lake at the kirov
then a swan trapped in ice is rescued
by ukrainian divers in dnipro river
you would thank them but the swan wing
of the vigilant fsb will send you barefoot
to siberia to freeze in some lake or another
when the swans in vienna are eaten
by hungry emigrants the duma applauds
rescuers save five year old stranded
on an inflatable swan on lake michigan
mother, please turn off the news

villonesque

he's a bulgarian i'm a turk
that potbellied stove
holds our circle by the feet
covered in seven pairs of dirty socks
just like our unwashed bodies (since the spring)
balled cotton in our hairy pits
funny old hats piled on our heads
shredded sandpaper underwear
filed down teeth razor cuts into skin
cold beneath bony ribs (what few remain)
clank bbrr brrr a knot of oak pops
sets our frozen wings on fire
the cinder blinds us smoke fills the lungs
if we knew all the wounds the future held
we would have excused us from being born
oh nuclear winter oh françois villon
where did all the healthy young people go?

brain drain cannon fodder 2024

one million russians fled russia to the west
taking their educated brains with them
leaving one hundred forty million free to breathe
the brainless air until half of them die
from not overthinking a war stalin would
have laughed at the way we poets laugh
at a massacred word in a pompous sentence
when the subject is millions only solzenitsin
could use enough words to impress stalin's
successors until putin put an end to that
and accounting for inflation dreams billions

we are the wrong size

we now live in canada   everything fits

all shoes were black and hurt
fading blue skirts gray hats
the wedding funeral suit
grandmother's wedding tulle
mr. fischer the tailor charged
little and fixed everything
what tailors we had then!
our new shoes needed iron
horseshoes for ice and snow
mr. blacksmith the ferrier
made sure our shoes were heard
steel on ice can sound forever
what ice we had! what snow!
the worser the things the better!
so much better we were then!
we wore each others's clothes!
girls borrowed each others's dresses
and boys wore their brothers pants!
we lived in our friends and cousins
we were so much closer then!

margareta

the village cows come home tired
sounding their dull bells
the blue snow pulls down the night
we wake before the sun
ice crunches under our horseshoed boots
we milk the cows the buckets overflow
cats lick the spillage in the furry shadows
we slosh the buckets to the kitchen where
Margareta scrubs us before breakfast
turns the sizzling bacon and the pain perdu
she dreams that she has gone to the Black Sea
where she turns over like a pancake
in the hot sun hungry for a mountain girl
brown on one side still white on the other
she didn't hear the get-to-the-shelter siren
for now it snows and milk boils in the past

forgetting then and now

Mobs of bored nomads swept over Europe setting fire to churches and universities. Captured nomads built firewalls to make the next nomads pause. After a short pause the new nomads breached the walls. They kept coming back to make new bonfires.

The old nomads asked the new nomads to not set fire to churches and universities so that the nomads sure to follow won't have to remember what they already set on fire.

Yes, but what's the fun in that, said Attila, I keep a thousand scribes to keep track of things we set fire to, but they lose their records or die or set themselves on fire. You can't trust anyone these days. Now we live in a new Digital Dark Ages brought about by info-nomads who drown in the memories of hard drives before they can even start an honest fire. We would be now as amnesiac as the 12th century arsonists.

Attila is such a fuss-budget.

The screens of the still-smoking empires soothe neo-barbarians to sleep. It's not history that repeats itself it's the (pixellated) memory of hot mayhem

cavafy

without nursing the hope of barbarians
cavafy would have died of boredom
and then they came hélas and they were worse
than the bourgeois in their cafe chairs
cavafy's profound ennui and unspent violence
fell to the blade of greater cosmic conformity
whose first victims were cultured jews
europe without jews was a nasty place a grimm
fairy tale alexandria burning in real time
an approximate home for l'homme approximatif
a dueling ground for shadows
loving your murderer was such a christian thing
even jesus had his doubts about it hence the fury
setting in motion the history of gangs
monastic orders motor clubs dark gyms poetry salons
even the smallest gang the cubists with only two core members
lost count of suicides and murders
to quarrel in the cafe for style is one thing
to kill your neighbors for dactyls another
to be a poet is to remember things that haven't yet
happened even when faced with catastrophic loss
the memory of hope for barbarians who come
to burn alexandria to the ground again
when wake in caves they smell the poet's yearning
they will be here again for the flesh and flames

how to live under fascism

I wear the uniform of your occupation
I am the nurse who walks with great aplomb
with soft shoes crisp white bonnet and a bomb
in my leather bag I've come to see the colonel
he hurts from signing warrants sitting on his ass
black coats, let me get through these doors!
I have a match and kerosene I need to see the boss
I think of it every time I drag my chains to work

my prisons

i went in socrates I came out plato
martial arts marital arts
i went in cool I came out square

i went in clueless
i came out stupid

the steel shutter music
bounced off the tin table
fat lips bent over gristle

all entry no exit
i will refuse fluids, right?

the dog days of summer 2001

we lay down on the bottom of the canoe
stupefied by eternity
we forgot the towers
anthrax
the neutron bomb

you were a data entry
grunt no more
and i no dada bouncer

the dragonflies mating on your back
flashed irridiscent blue
with the current

i was a young fool
you were a young fool too

memory

i forgot the secret
places but the keys
are there
also the passports
and the plane tickets
we are en route
passing through the
walls
i trip over your
comma you hold on
to my coda
disguised like
peaceful cows at the
border
between a yiddish
joke and the
burlesque

retouching

several times a day my mother
retouched her studio photographs
to hide what in the people of those days?

wrinkles of worry
black eyes of working men's fists
eyes that couldn't remember to open
smiles that came from broken mirrors
brides in the blanched chiffon
of three drunken days in a life
as long as the exposure before the lens
of the camera with its black curtains
for the identity cards to be stamped
at the gates of the mustard gas plant
their grooms in olive army gear
soon to burst like pimples under fire
in uniforms too big inherited from elders
brushed with the flour of patriotic rhyme
trampled by starving mules in the muddy blood
of the same ideal pasture in its iodine blue
cardboard frame suggesting the light of heaven
for the inspired corpses of next time

retouching 2

mother took off her panicked gear
removed the rose-colored glass the party
installed in her camera

the detroit police replaced it with an eye
that watched me turn from an alien
who doesn't like to be photographed
into a cover girl for Life magazine

america is the difference between aliens
and satirists from the pink glass that shatters
utopias of the twentieth century
and the light of reproach bodies stream out of

obvious and sad to me in my rainy grey childhood
at the borders of three empires
my mother had to be a survivor
so that I might become a class traitor

teaching in a time of war

for anton yakovlev

class, take this "constructive criticism"
and turn it into constructions from objects
found among your classmates
combs switchblades pills baggies lucky beads
worn talismans smudged phone #s from nights
in alleys and ruins   doodles of hearts and bodies
to be collaged with eyeliner and rouge
fidgeting in wait for the shelter sirens
a way to keep your hands busy doing
something else than jerking off machine guns
you are waiting for the mobiles and tears to ring
in your flesh   there is no hurry   there is no hurry
the unsent postcards in the pockets of dead soldiers
"my love, it is a good thing that you are not here"
panic from head to toe no one can stand still for the future
the anesthetic pleasure machine in every house
not yet built never to be built
a bomb crater to raise your children in
class, phone your dreams in to the auction of pain
agitate your lives while you still have them
reward your constructivist randomness
in the mild breeze blood flows from the earth
into your empty bellies
class, be not ruffled by the esthetic payoff
the pinpricks of pleasure from your spiky straight-jackets
european culture decimates you
and diagrams your sentence
your constructivist examples will hang where you will

hair in my work

A concordance of my poetry reveals a lot of hair, a tall hairstack reaching above the Viennese-cake-style excesses of the French court or Elizabeth Taylor's Hair Babel. My high school history teacher, Comrade Sausage, sent me to the barber to shorten what I grew in the image of the Beatles I had never seen. I returned shaved smooth and disrupted the teaching of the conquest of Dacia by Emperor Trojan in 106 CE. Laughter roiled the classroom through the boys' regulation crewcuts and the girls' shoulder-length tresses. The boys' breton was styled after Roman soldiers' for twenty centuries. The Roman conquerors abandoned Dacia in 275 C.E, but their haircut stayed behind, first as fear of legions' return, then as pride of kinship. History class did not go well after that: the manual became outdated, our teacher grew sideburns, the dictator outlawed the Beatles and had his own son captured by the police at a nude beach on the Black Sea. The police clipped him to regimental correctness. The hair wars were just beginning in the West then. They were already fought fiercely in the commie kingdoms. From the first airing by Radio Free Europe of "I Wanna Hold your Hand" communism hung by its hair over the bottomless garbage-can of history until it fell in. After it fell, hair sprouted at the same rate that the Carpathian mountains were deforested by capitalism. The commie post-collapse hair was not political hair, but hair nostalgic for an epoch when it loved the woods. Hair is the axis of history: the Iron Curtain was the Hair Curtain, nineteen centuries were bearded, the clean-shaven half of the twentieth century grew hair in mass graves, but the second half was long-haired and hopeful. I am bald now, but when the cloud dissipates I'll get a powdered wig and become Hair Judge at the Court of Pan, the hairiest god

Dear Ovid nicknamed The Nose

Milenia passed since your letters of lament
about barbarians reeking of garlic
and the bonechiller winds that cut
to the bone through your thin coat

your sad verses read slowly at the court
made the emperor's wife cry from laughing
even her bodyguards rolled with merriment
at your begging permission to return to Rome

they knew that Tomis your city of exile
had stadiums theatres and fine schools
the local girls knew your poetry by heart
and the barbarians excelled for the empire

what fine detail you revealed in the verses
your Roman fans loved and for this reason
wanted you to stay in your exile and keep
making immortal this form of manifest absence

Where is yesteryear CNN's *Poppy*?

For N. Stoie and F. Villon

The late ice age hadn't quite ended when lyric poetry began.
Je suis François Villon né à Pontoise I'd like another hot toddy.
They say now that in less than a hundred years it will be safe
To go out again at night and find a new kind of lice and heat.
The late ice age ended but the lyric didn't hear the news.
Catholics still massacre protestants everybody massacres the Jews.
And still it is cold in the sad hearts of poets and flaneurs.
The fleurs du mal came and went and became other fleurs.
Even in our time when we are fat and sloppy we draw close in pubs
And ask "whatever in the world happened to CNN's Poppy?"
CNN Poppy's face was like a hungover flower that said every night:
"What I mistake! Only if I could! I said pregnant! And I might!"
She meant pragmatic. And then she is gone. Where ah where is Poppy?
Where did she go? Did she shave her head, abandon the Republic?
Without CNN's Poppy what will become of the honest body public?
What will our body public do without CNN's Poppy? Let's get it right.
We must at all cost go out in the cold to cherchez la femme.
We should follow el cash but please let's no longer tarry in this dive.
If we don't get fractional voting we'll never get out of here alive.
We'll have twitter monarchy worse that the snows of the tzar.
Tired of toxic language and the only voice that made us happy,
inheritors of the small fortune left to us after the world went pixel
we must find Poppy's wonder medicine of charm before nightfall.
It snows again and more than sunlight we miss our evening Poppy.
Ah where is CNN's Poppy in this miserable medieval year?
Everyone with an account at this bank of sorrow get in line.
Come closer here and drink on this perilous perch and shaky porch.
Where is yesteryear's Poppy, the CNN lady with the torch?
She must have gone away on a boat, Air France is on strike.
Ah where where in the snowy sky is our televised liberty Poppy?

stockholm mussea

for eva leonte

at the stockholm museum of modern art
swedish actors stand in front of
romanian art by marcel janco
victor brauner and constantin brancusi

declaiming in actor voices in english
translation from the work of the artists'
poet friends tzara fondane blaga cassian

nobody warned tourists that an alien
music awaited them turkish slavic
german hungarian english free concert

from museum closets that are safe rooms
built behind masterworks
to shield curators from angry masses
masked actors surge like swat teams

the stew of foreign vocables and sighs
has been rehearsed with a robust budget
souffleurs in the chandeliers even hold
first editions to wind up our thespians

it's a surprise afternoon for lifetime subscribers

indoor shower in cool stockholm breeze

diversity does include fainting
by harried elders who fought a war or two
and still carry shrapnel in in their flesh

but for the children pupils on vacation
who drank bravely the night before
the genii of art and verse encourage romance

few experiences compare with
swallowing the castor oil of modern art

malfunctioning angels fast-forward
the motor of art in their fresh bodies
athletic urban even in translation

on wheels of modern art
1896 1914 1921 1931 2015 2024
moving into the future before
the once-in-seventeen-years cicadas of war
prepare the materia prima for new art
train new cannon-fodder

take a joyous bath in diversity
children, before your watchers
interrupt the lassitude of your ce-cream
afternoon in this civilised city

the zeitgeist is obscure and angry

fondane

i am fondane fruit of a tree that grew from mystic mud
of rural yiddish belt of earth between the mountains
reader of medieval torah and romantic verse
more jewish than rabbi zwi more romanian than bacovia
more french than de gourmont more shaken than an american
cocktail in a sheep's skull more existential than shestov
I lead my long-haired cows with heavy udders over peaks
of clover to the sea my bulls more golden my fields more fragrant
my grasses more nutritious than the figs of the euphrates
these vessels are mine, mariners, i am fondane,
my epics will power your sails for all the coming times
i am the wandering jew and greek ahaserus ulysses and fondane

tzara fondane celan

my dear anthologies
of gifts and misfortune
birth dates emigration dates
urgent breaks between wars
what is the plural of hiatus
illusions of freedom within
where the holes of culture used to be
now overgrown by words
tzara's good timing
the radical temperament of youth
your fucking bourgeois hypocrisy must die
fondane's bad timing
longing for summer pastures
i do mistake the pastoral for culture
these are my sheep
celan in the silence
after the apocalypse
translates the murmur
of the murdered mother tongue

a tool

This is the cradle
inside which new york, hong kong, and peking
squeeze with a shriek
to fuse into the
corporate baby. Who has, again,
fooled the jews and is running
upstream. Mao shears sheep
and grins in wait.

max blecher

max blecher exiled by TB from his flesh
exults in a discus thrower's body
lit by the well-being of athletic youth
ecstatic magnet to his incomplete reality
in max's world nothing is trivial or weary
we the unsick in our mindless health
will never know the force of such body swap
we die unaware of the force of self at war
with its sinew even as the faces of world war
press against the hospital windows
max dies at twenty-eight years of age
not older than us healthy prodigies headed
for the gas chambers
a lucky Jew who died in 1938
before his ill body lost his light body

everything turns into a museum

the more heinous the history the more popular the museum
take europe for example
that stuff is all shrunken heads
curated to read like the newspaper
the smoked ham of ethnic cuisine
next visit we must take our country cousins
to the city and leave them in the vitrines
the next generation must learn fine dying

the avantgarde then and now
for Valery

The problem with being ahead of your time is that you're eventually going to get there again with everybody else and experience extreme ennui. I mean, there is no way to be ahead of your time in your mind and take your body along. Your body has to get there with every other body, and when it does, your mind goes, yeah right, been there, done that. This is chiefly the problem with the virtual world we are moving into: we don't know where we are going as we tap on glass and wheel our arms in the make-believe world. Here are a few things that are going away: the flesh minus fingers and arms and maybe an eye. In the memory box that you will recover postmortem, is the physical proof of your creation, your solitary pursuits, your freedom to be anonymous, your own chosen speed, your fuzzy fringes, the right to be boring, and the pleasure or embarrassment of changing your mind. All your effects before you were incarcerated have been inventoried when you went in. Kidney, lungs, ID, wallet, brain. All hands and eyes to the shower. And then to work. In the old meat-world you layed hands on things and used your senses to feel them, and then smash them to hard bits if you felt like it, or love them to death like a sweaty Samoyed in New Orleans in July. No more. You belong to the keyboard now. The word you type is more coherent than you ever were. Subdue the memory of your undisciplined incoherence to the alphabet. You are now so enchanted with worlds constructed by grammar engineers that you don't know how to get back to the one made by the crazy gods. You forget the funny goop that spewed you out in the first place. It isn't any great shakes predicting the future, but it's a real drag living in it. My first reality-replacement was the light-switch in our apartment: I turned it on and it wasn't night anymore. For the longest time, I could live with that, keeping two contradictory realities in mind: it was night and it was day, it was dark and it was light at the same time. But those realities started looking sinister when they began to exchange places: I flipped a switch to make it dark at night, and vice-versa. The reality-replacing machine made things interesting at first. But now I'm all there, all fingers arms and eyes. Where is my mind and body. Where is my vitamin D? I know it's still day and night for animals, so maybe I'll just turn into a Samoyed, OK. There is no such thing as an avant-garde body. Suicide is the only avantgarde

any habit

We are nuns in habits any habits
We don't need any more wisdom or any more foolishness
We have cloth for a thousand years

the uses of the berlin wall

everyone agrees that the old Berlin Wall
was a congealed mass of putrified vomit
and it stank to heaven
good riddance

and yet we must erect
a new Berlin Wall
between humans and the deep fakes we spew
out of the uncanny valley ad astram

the old Wall exacted a great price for blue jeans
used to practice je m'en fou
all exertion no choice

i don't love shopping it's exhausting
nostalgia-imbued deep fakes confuse the animal
hunting for something perilous
a purple language with meat in the vowels

whenever I don't hear from somebody
I assume that i am pregnant

the therapist I don't have said to me
why don't you check in with yourself.
i used thermometers thermoses thermal probes imaging machines
introspection dictation distortion enactment by puppets
religions buried in secret bones in my astral body
the filthy mouths of my youth's bullying multilinguals
when i finally reached myself it turned out
that I was pregnant with twins who were themselves
pregnant with twins writing with lipstick
on the mirrors of time

new word ordinance

Language the virus gives one logorhea but I found the vaccine that renders one mute, or at least limits the number of words one speaks to five per week. Siri can you make them shut up? Yes, henceforth you people will be born with 10,000 words per lifetime allowance. It's up to you how many and how fast you use them. A profligate like this writer can use them all in one day and be silent for the rest of his life. Swedes who use words sparingly to save calories can make them last a lifetime. If you die with a number of unused words, you can leave them to your heirs. Look at all these rich kids in the cafe yada yada, all inherited. One of them just used her lifetime quota before I finished my capuccino. A yellow leaf fell from a tree in my coffee. It must be Fall. Where the talk leads only the money that silently follows knows

my yoga teacher cassandra

has only good news for my body
and for my mind she warms them
and she becalms them unlike her
greek namesake who left her
listeners terrified and tense
ah the onomastic turnaround
took twenty centuries to turn
the older story on its head
which explains ex-lingua why
my modern body feels comfort
in the new diachronic goddess

clara

She is the anarchist in the room
She biked here through twelve small towns
wheeling so in her wake the wind was rough.
Locals felt the mal vents the spring airs.
They dreamt that they were living in the Alps.
One Alp in particular sang in their lungs.
She sold the bike to the movies and was film.
Trains passing in the daytime did nothing
for her. "Something went to war and bit me"

haifa

it's amazing how little ennui I'm capable of
i'm climbing the built-by-my-inability-to-drink wall
on the other side are three countries at war
and a placid sea drinking the shadows of olive trees
to feed its blueness to the chatter of fish
from submarines portholes the apocalypse
counts the steps of the baha'i gardens
within missile range israel is my age
it's all the things I am minus US citizenship
if there is a place to be serious this may be it

cousins

i feel tenuous and fragile my cousin tells me
she is a doctor in tel aviv
tenuous and fragile behind the mask
she wears now twenty hours a day
like the memory of the endless meetings of her communist
youth when she had to keep her mouth shut
when our faces were masks and we never said what we thought
and whenever she hears the word "border"
her mask suffocates her even more
like the barbed wire borders of our country back then
where we escaped from through a miracle
to the terrifying borders of the promised lands
always under imminent threat
"if you don't believe in miracles here you are not reasonable"
                              (ben gurion)

the border and the mask do not separate
her from now or then
her tenuous fragility is not just the human condition
our mothers lived through world depression
and world war where their lives meant nothing
to the country they loved despite their people
the mask and the border are our only defenders
behind our hidden mouths and changing borders
fragility and tenousness
are coiled snakes ready to strike

hello future healers!
for tristan

hello parents and kin of future healers
your children have already healed something in you
something that all people need
what really ails us is what also ails the water the earth the air
the plants and the creatures we share

young healers your job is big
personal death cannot be healed
nor does it need to be

maybe you young'uns can heal even that
but don't do it
this body of mine does not need to be here forever

tender your care to what ails our commons

refuse the palliatives of incomplete science
choose the entirety of being
a creature that is not a machine
a large organism relentlessy alive and evolving

you are courageous and thus obligated
to be teachers of courage

the good news is that there is personal death
but no universal death
the good news is that there is love

beware of riches
your immeasurable riches are inside you
the result of two billion years of evolution

everything that ever lived is contained in you

courage is the world's true currency

so what is political poetry?

rhetoric refusing its prior premise?
a proud being asking for what's not his?
a penniless libertarian at the free library?
the ceo who is an echo of himself?
the exceptionalist in norm core shorts?
the ghost bug squished on the glass plate?
socialism in its verbal youth?
cosmogony drafted from metaphors of justice?
executives of the freedom to loiter?
accidental rhymes in the park of headless statues?
dusty podiums and second-hand microphones?
boredom wearing clothes from the movies?
hearts stirred with icecream sticks of first love?
toy guns pointed at robots with pocket nukes?
or neruda mixing vodka with rum at the congress bar?
i could go on but I've been left alone in the car

lecture

thank you for being here
we are all connected with the screen
behind the dressing screen
you are changing into a dragon
how did the avantgarde end up in the past?
it fell in love with the enemy
& when it shared its info with the mainstream
it sank into its empty gas balloons
weighted with the lead of regret
now i watch her vintage charms on glass

one-liner

i write an equation & i meet a polemic

dissecting aliens

the alien has no center it is the center
looking for something to take its place
the alien's chief desire is to be dissected
into stories told by numbers and voila
its wish comes true in the dry black box
that once held a wet globe of doubt

The Shoe and the Refrigerator

by Codrescu/La Fontaine

Artificial Ignorance and Augmented Intelligence set up camp
in the moonlit brain of a lonely humanity on a little planet.
The people on the little planet welcomed them enthusiastically
at first. I mean, who doesn't love a refrigerator talking to a shoe?
When the refrigerator locked the shoe inside and it wouldn't open
some people were annoyed but called it a glitch and called someone
who obliged for a fee to free the shoe from the fridge.
When the cell phone talked directly to the fridge to free the shoe
the people stood by and watched in wonder and said nothing
though the shoe was cold when it was freed and it hurt the foot.
Then the shoe started talking to the refrigerator and to the phone
and completely ignored the people who still grinned and suffered.
It was only when their shoes started pulling the people inside
refrigerators and keep them until they froze to death
that the thought just before freezing occurred to some that perhaps
all this intelligence did more harm than good. It was too late.
Nobody walked in the snow outside where the AI birds chattered.

AI is the biggest vampire

eat your heart out Nosferatu
suck this Dracula
shoo bats from our attics
away with all you giggolos
silence your midnight choir
we have no need of you we have
the biggest and best bloodsucker

circling the drain

I don't like big data. It might seem that big data is indifferent to my opinion, but this isn't the case. See the blurred face on the advertising billboard: AI knows my face and blurred it. Not for privacy. AI will blur every digitized human face. After people's privacy on public transportation or buses and streets was abolished by cameras, the image industry moved on to make my face every face. This face will be blurred of all conceivable features for all conceivable futures

Subject: New Friend Requests

I would like to confirm your friend request, but once again FB (Fat Book) has cut me off at 5,000. FB must think that more than 5,000 people cuts into its zuckerberg (sugar mountain), and becomes a Gang. OK, then. Migrate your request to the AC (Andrei Codrescu Gang) and we'll act accordingly, like a mob at a DR (Dada Rave.) Our voices bounce in the glass prison rising from the poop holes of muskrats and there is a rush to the final dam on the river algorhytm of suspects my friends thank you for breaking the polite loyalties of the past. Let's roam the trash heaps of history picking up perfectly good frames dripping with honey from the primitive hives we keep busy buzzing

flat is dead

new orleans late night zen pickup reroutes me gently above molly's where a motley crew of gutter-punks are drawing cross-legged on the tilted floor, writing with colored chalk on blackboard walls, making paper birds and rag dolls to place in uneven boxes nailed to the walls, or lying down on the hardwood floors reading. their dogs, mostly rottweilers, but also german shepherds and dachsunds, lie quietly beside their busy owners, some of them chained to tattooed arms. it's 4 am in the french quarter. it's not flat

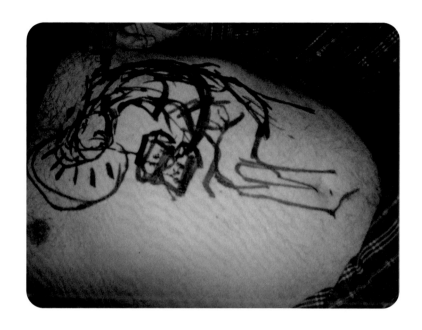

never naked

'ourobouros' on the small of your back
sparkles its sequins bright enough to read
the haiku lettered around your waist
spring flows with the moon
shadow of poet in her glow
hears winter ahead
roaming animates your private weather
the icy winds and snow your living cinema
reanimate what you like
long lines of ghosts wait in the snow
with eyes of popcorn and degrees in film
to enter the theater closed for decades now

how no money becomes money

In 1974 Free Box Chic meant taking clothes out of the free box in front of the co-op in Monte Rio. A year later the free clothes were put back in the free box. The connoisseurs who took them out on the second round found them ultra-chic. All the holes were in the right places. Not long after, holey free jeans became scarce, as did the free box ethos. Young people bought new jeans, then tore holes in them. It wasn't long before hole-making assembly lines were manned by immigrants who found the clothes ridiculous. It was the Reagan era of hole-making jobs. In the countries they came from, the only people with holes in their pants, were beggars. Knee holes suggesting that the fabric was worn by performing oral sex, horrified immigrants from catholic countries who had spent their childhood on their knees praying for work in America. Making holes in american pants was not the job they prayed for. Not only were they alienated from their product, like Karl Marx said, they were enraged by it. That is the wonderful thing about America: you can hate the thing you're making even if you don't know what it is, because sooner or later you'll wear it. The transition from hippie free-box holes-twice-worn to factory-ripped holes took only enough time to employ three generations of americans. And that's how no money became money. And social evolution saw people travel through the holes in their jeans from misery to luxury, from refuge to residency, from necessity to fashion. The free eden of holey hippie jeans became the memory of fantasy, aka advertising. The executive of ripping reigned in the nation of holes. The zeitgeist authorized the nation to make and sell what didn't exist. The logic of missing fabric had equivalents in language. Articles and conjunctions went missing. To speak with holes while wearing ripped jeans was the new language. Subjectivity vanished through holes leaving behind the suggestion of an activity that had once been perilous. Flesh looked out of these holes with google eyes at knee or buttock level. Sometimes smoke came out of the flesh under the holes like fumaroles and nobody minded paying for it, not even the hole makers who spent their money on the holes they made

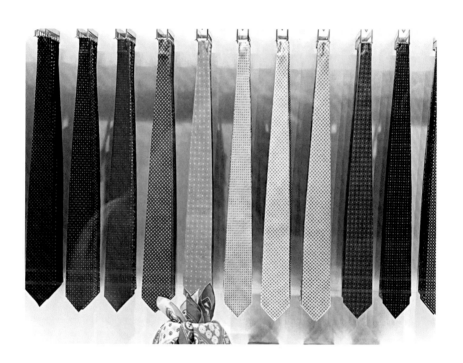

passing pipes along peacefire

when i was a hippie
and i was never hippie
it sounded like happy
and I was anything but
i was occasionally ecstatic
and often angry
but one time in in san francisco
in the mid 20th century
in a house of silent vegetarians
at a commune in the haight
i held hands with two jeunes filles en fleur
who were the reason i was a hippie
and sucked deeply on a pipe still wet with
the golden saliva the foam of aphrodites
on my left and on my right
and i regreted eating the kale and brown rice
because they nearly obliterated the taste
of their divine lips but the trace was enough
to keep me up all night in a kitchen chair
at the window covered with paper flowers
writing a poem in french in the hope
that one of them would slip out of the ziggurat
of bodies in the communal bedroom
and tiptoe nude to me to ask what i was
writing and i imagined that she sat on my lap
while the sap of poetry met the foam of her
and this is what happened they both came
out of the bedroom and tiptoed past me
to some german guy sleeping with his head
on the other window sill and they coiled
like serpents around him and made godly music
he was a real hippy i was just a poet writing in french

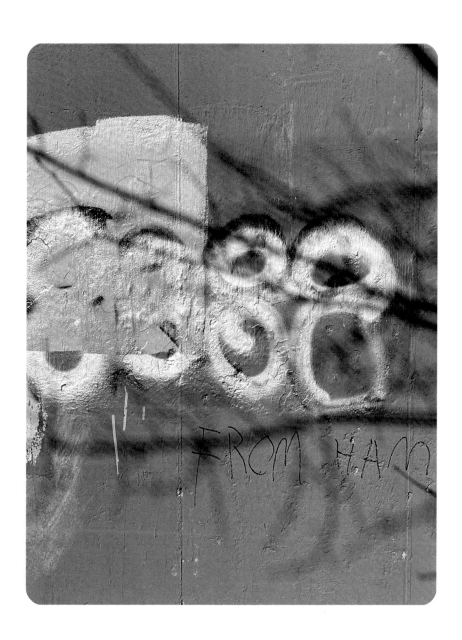

the junk paraphernalia of others

I no longer need the world
still a sandwich would be nice

we must walk slow
like caterpillars on the shady side of the street
because it's saturday and we are hungover

the freedom of monkeys

i escaped from the zoo
to a beastly utopia
that looked a lot like america
intoxicated by its own myths
made in holywood
king kong the leader of our nation
swaps his flask with me

we buy time & sleep

if you are wasting yourself on futile chase
we will buy your time
satisfactory payoff in brain jolts

are you sleeping too much?

here at the insomnia society
we purchase your dreams
your inarticulate maps of life
for simple directions to bed

we mix your time & dreams in a vat
boiling the magma of the future
we sell as it bubbles up crystals

finger on the app

what once was a whisper
is a broadcast now

each person is a platform
for ears close enough to bite

oh princess-telephone u yawp
in past party-line long distance

now your everyone platform
jumps into a million ears

so what's secret if we all know it
even as earwax blinds my tears

cannot do again we did that last
to ghost you is a duty to the past

everybody was always a platform
the darkness was a palimpsest of ears

everybody had to be careful
to say the opposite of what they thought

it was the only way to stay a citizen
it doesn't matter now it is too late

if you're not a fake
show me the pills you take

what was a whisper
is a broadcast now

posted in the window

it takes ten dogs to clone
your beloved pooch Ondine

first you must skin her
to make furry muffs for the staff

then you must dissolve tissue
from her eyes to make eyes

we tell you this so you can think
before we start to clone Ondine

we give you a day to let this sink in
signed by the staff
of Clone Your Own Dog Inc

catalyst speed thing up

it moves a seed an idea it quickens an incipience it inverts abstraction it shapes nebulous thought it takes vagueness to material makes the ideal into the practical it translates the surreal into the real the real into the hypereal
induces catharsis   pull the trigger

baudelairesques

1. the clerkaverse

timing is important to our secular hive
because we all au fond believe the lie
that an angel with a stopwatch hovers
above each one of us keeping time until we die

then the angel moves on to the dead's ex
rewarded with a better timepiece maybe a rolex
containing more time because widowed humans
live longer and in the future people live longer
and longer until the bored angels incarnate
into the humans who died on their watch
these humans are immortal oh my crotch
oh my nard syringe my apostate prostheses

above our secular hive lives nobody now
emptied of angels the timepieces run on sand
keeping time for ex-angels straining to believe
that their old forms still hold them in hand

2. queneauonion

what little dignity there was in pain transfered
in writing on a keyboard from the tips of flesh
you brushed past me that evening in Lorraine
I hurled my Olivetti into the trash sea

watched waves of plastic pour past every key

I jumped from screen to screen before you
finished dawn's honeydew over my half-writ aubade
I left my iphone in your bed heard the distant horse
of your returning knight after he killed all my alters

What little dignity there was in writing
with a chewed pencil in a lined notebook
moved to an order where the pencil was all chewed
and my imaginary dignity blew away whatever humility
the dandelion graphite ceded to the keyboard
and I suffered from hubris and the loss
of the end of line page chapter
brevity sense syntax now gone completely
until the iPhone called hullo? why all the work?

Viewing the junk paraphernalia of youth and seed
the poetry fades unraveled thread of castle in disarray
of letter demons lighting inside morning's melted head

pleasures of the plague

i came back to the old reading habit
after an internet bath
i had to take a several showers after

and oh lord

I felt like a relapsing addict going back
to the first hit of his old vice
elated and high and filled to the brim with pleasure
and guilt of course
woe to the gambler
who wins that first hand!

the gateway drug was the dialogue of the dogs
and these two dogs were meat on the bone
of my starving brain
the death of ivan illich
and bartleby the scrivener
MORE MORE MORE
fanfarlo by charles baudelaire! please!
the parasol of best flasks and baggies
more marvelous and cheaper than drugs
flew off bookshelves with pages fluttering
dying to be fed and petted
by the storm of hungry cats i loosened

do I have enough to last me for the rest of my life
if when god forbid this pandemic ends it?
i feed my starving zoo
a happy mix of robotussin and anselm hollo

and to think the internet pretended to be me!

tenses

the future's when a guy points a gun at you
and says you're history
the past is if you're the guy with the gun
the gun is always present

it was there when i was born before
the gunshot wedding and it was there
when my mother hid it under the pillow
to use in case hungarian bandits came
on a sleepless night over the border
to finish what they started before

guns greeted us to america in detroit
from tank turrets enforcing curfew
obligating me to falsify for myself
a license to carry a gun good forever

moses (mosi)

baskets are hanging from the branches
of a new tree growing in front of the grotto
where i sleep when i don't want to be found
each basket has a heavy severed head in it
that sways in the cold northern wind
from each basket a name tag and a flag
whips back and forth in the rising wind
i am startled to find my name calligraphed
on the coif of a prussian soldier's head
i tried counting the baskets but gave up
when the snow covered the jungfrau

theories are fascist

the greeks didn't make up their gods to serve jung
archetypes are the transport of gods for theory
that mess of gods and their weird stories
served anybody who needed them for anything
the gods lived in disorder just like their humans
got drunk and fucked each other with music
jung's ordered gods march behind dividing psyches
counting each beat with a sober face and a worn story
frozen icons exhuding the miasmas of misplaced glory
the real gods are still misbehaving in nameless groves
out of print immortals with unprintable stories

the old days

in new york in the late 60s of the last century there was downtown and uptown uptown they had taste and money downtown we were against those things though some money would have been nice but we were definitely against taste we had our own in the lower east side I once gave david peele $10 from my boss at the paperback booksmith to ask him to take his damn band away from our corner because he was scaring our customers with his awful song 'we are from the lower east side and we don't care if we live or we die' we did care a little but my boss was all about money coming downtown was called slumming i got george plimpton to come to the lion's head to discuss my story for the paris review and fayette hickox george's assistant said that's the farthest downtown george came in twenty years we were in the west village mind you the bourgeois side of the village i personally considered cooper square the farthest border of my world and the beginning of empire where a suit was required a suit i occasionally borrowed i'm bringing up these quaint notions because the topos of this age has obscured the patch separating down from up now teeming with jillions of art graduates art majors art administrators art critics and other nonnative species the postmortem life of a corpse killed by art maggoty abundance efflorescence real estate speculation ... we artists have worked hard at killing art for most of the 20th century but the dang thing keeps raising its head from duchamp's pissoir and warhol's soup can spraying evenly the flat color canvas of corporate perfection

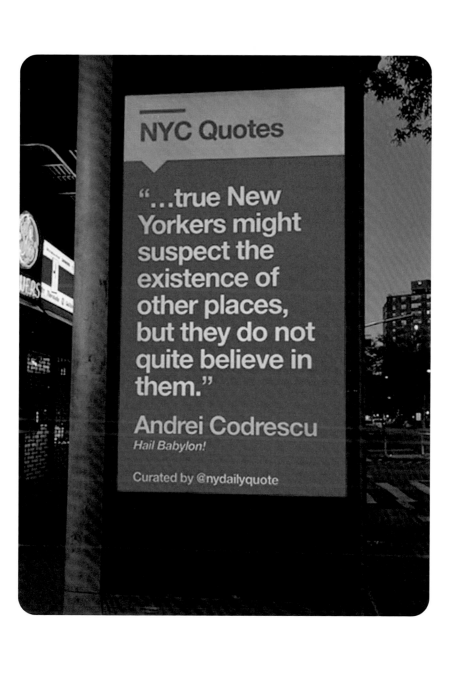

us & them

to us it's a house of mirrors.
to them a glass house
you wonder why they throw stones?

who done it

god is the lone survivor. marcus texts from the twin towers memorial: "meet you by the lone survivor tree." sho' enough. after the visit I text laura: "remember when you called me to the tv in baton rouge when the first plane hit? and remember that in martinique we saw the picture of the last survivor of the volcano eruption that destroyed the city of st. pierre? He was the drunk in the jail. maybe there is a always a lone survivor. after katrina, the wwoz's radio katrina, a beloved voice, left the city in onomastic shame. since human history is an uninterrupted chain of disasters, god is the designated survivor. but did he do it? yes, he was drunk on the q train to jamaica, and it took no time at all

three at the bean

tired of language & personae
& the inheritors of small fortunes
at the bean across from the strand
two blue-jeaned jeunes filles
one french the other argentine
pink scarf silver rings pricey jeans
cortazar sticking out of french bag
discuss going to jfk to fly to paris
where two husbands and quatre enfants
wait for them with a mountain of laundry!
air france is on strike! it's a lie
they want to stay in new york
it is time for the ship intellectual penis
to lay anchor by the strand and i hear:
"and because air france is on strike
we must climb on board and pose for jackson"
it feels good to write a nouveau roman
in the bean where we now lie on the floor
on peruvian llama skins under a single flame of sentiment
burning in a shell under a winking cyclops eye
yes we must revolt now we say in one telepathic sigh
our existence is on strike like air france it can
fall apart at the same speed in what is not the bean
yes we must perform and do nothing about it
every place not new york is a brake inertia stasis
e pure si muove must banish
whatever moves against what it is made of

in my second sleep

i was a newspaper
flat and looking for typos
the guide to the afterlife
was in times new roman
on the page i was scanning
like an ant with a magnifying glass
somebody's obituary said
your sins become virtues after you die
so make sure you sin a lot
when you're alive
i thought of this after i woke up
the page i was on stayed in my sleep
the lost technologies live in dreams
extinct birds of old habits

new york date

beards come back when men are useless
eating out is expensive
dishes are small the food sucks
you want to save some for later
beards are takeout bags
an aftersex snack is what sex
is all about i empty my beard
isn't a nite in new york worth living here for?
i wish i was a lesbian in 1968

parachute song

all my life I fought with capitals
while living in them

the best human gift is perspective
it's also the worst
when calling for a closeup

it is a gift only when it employs
minimal distance between
what you see and what looks back

we have a school for teaching
appropriate distance
it's called a slum a favella

how long do I have to stay away

the circumstance is a circus stance
without circus the city is a limp gag

with the circus you can take a stance
my clown but you will rarely get paid

regaining Solace with flashback RX

Calm is something from the last century
and even then it lasted only minutes before
it turned into angst rage or demonic laughter.
The last daylong calm to last a day
was for me in the 14th century when I was a monk.
It was the result of a monastic practice
that was like a rowboat on rough seas
back on shore for a spell and a drink.
I also have a memory of it from 1963 when we didn't have tv.
I don't believe those models are still available
but you can try this now: make a box easy to open.
Make sure there is absolutely nothing inside
then crawl in and think you're Fell Swoop magazine.

poetry road

the dog days of summer
when we lied down
on the bottom of the canoe
stupefied by eternity

sufficed
why did i leave that infinite
to become a dada bouncer
at your private club?

encroaching slime

don't worry
if you feel like saying fuck all the time
it's the slime in the ancient voting booths
the peepshows of yore
the slime of old futures
pouring their rhetoric
into your helpless finger
poking out of your urn
it isn't your right it's your turn
to taste the sticky memory
of your ancestors' ashes

same object different subject

Habit would drain the miraculous
if miracles weren't changelings.
People on the subway you see them
every day they are the exploded OED.
We'll see each other often if we look
sparingly: to be a one-off serial
is what I am working on, bloom tree

at the oyster bar

grecian formula and dippity doo
are waiting for aphrodite

embracing heritage terrorism

time happens when mother happens
art happens when time carries pieces of you
to the trash that passes for a hill in ft lauderdale

all your theories are in that heap there
where the city dumps the ash of your people

a river a of money flows into the mausoleum
of investors in pain and out into landing pads
for their freeways intercoastal ufos

the indifferent force takes your toys
hurls them on the pretzels of toll roads
you are compelled to follow
like this poem you quit following ages ago

time is as thick as your knowledge of it
which is your knowledge of nothing
though you are beginning to glimpse
other rivers that share your stuff

love would be nice about here

needs

flat little paper people
$ baby food opium
1 nut with an aftertaste of detroit 1965

to us necessities are misspelling
giggle is our search engine
of all that is funny under attack

summer

won't you crawl
like a redhaired tarantula
all over my body?

note

Laughing at yourself means that somebody paid attention to you before you were five. This is the cut-off age for understanding adult sincerity. You were fortunate if they laughed sincerely at your goofiness and you laughed with them. The ability to see your own goofiness is the gift of adult sincerity. After that they give you nothing but grief

in the ginza

my earphones are life-savers
in the sea of drunk octopus
the confidence that my fingertips
are flesh not round plastic knobs
in a world designed for vertigo
is one blinking manga away
from many-punch berserk man
guys are manuals women technology
rouge calipers on black silver scales
girls come with double snow girl
dinosaur men trail long feathers
ornament and multiplication
speed up this urban rushing mind
my body is very very far behind

dance to the coming panic

girls swaying in the subway
laugh as if their bodies are accidents

the underground explodes
if you drunk-dance before things happen
you'll have no idea what happened
eight minutes from now in a dream

can you get a little more depressed please

i can but what would you get out of it?
you don't have to know
what the tracks are thinking
you cannot stop them
coming early was a reason to dance
and dancing was a must when it got
too late to leave
i caught a slice of you
you were beautiful
you had something
from last night in your eyes
and something from tomorrow
on your lips now hovering in the air

why does *sourire* have no english for it?

concretization of the cloud

his head said my mother is in the clouds
it is true
most of my young life my head
was in the clouds
it came briefly down to earth
in my teen years because that's where the girls were
on earth a scary place
the earth girls saw that my head was vaporous
on those rare occasions when it came out of the clouds
vapor terrified steamboats exploded
shapes and sounds no shore to anchor in
get your head out of the clouds
my mother my teachers and the girls
panic-prescribed and simultaneously called out
which caused my head to rise higher into the clouds
where it remained for long times in its trousers
in the company of majakovski
even now my head should you need it is in the clouds
but it no longer matters as it once did
since clouds have been sharing themselves with everyone
and earth joined it long ago in my youth

crossings

for Constance

so the question is : what do you do with a box of dead photographs?

the answer is: forget them.
and the other answer is the one you
so eloquently gave: no mystery, no dice.
and the other thing is:
i wrote you a poem on the plane.
i'm quoting a section:

"the pleasures
 of travel are due
  to the strange
     hours
   we keep to see them"

constance
   crossing time zones
     as easily as legs
sleeping undisturbed
with hundreds of strangers
 home everywhere
   and nowhere
your hours are where
we are all going to live
constance your name says it all
   there is a constant in the world
     a constancy
        consistency
indifferent to the maps
  & grids of past worlds
      forging ahead with the thread

of the human thing
the thread mr. your-name-on-hat uses to hand-sew the voltaire hat
   ariadne's thread
     but also penelope
       who waits even as she strays far into the labyrinth
       she weaves
         as she threads

constance fears heights
her favorite movie is vertigo
she threads water
holding the flag in the air
"don't thread on me"

life must seem fragmentary
   sometimes
but the thread you thread
   through time and space
is brilliant and visible
   it sparkles
     and can be seen from space
but also
   from below

hi, constance!

im so famous im sure im somebody else

a poor tuesday bohemian with a sunday attitude
a bohemian is a poor anybody with an attitude
having talent is nice you can sing for your supper
a wingless duck doesn't land cooked in your plate

you can write poetry for sixty years
publish and exhibit yourself shamelessly for fifty
words are the money of your face denomination
the minute you see another as 'yourself'
they become as boring as yourself

the street crazy shouts
"everything goes out the window!"
"what country should we bomb next?"
are you the funny poet who's written more serious lines
than all the masked puffy clowns prancing on zoom?
are you are the punk just kicked out of meta by expired visa?

the internet is a loaded gun in the hands of a three year-old
a syntax of desperate struggle with bad toilet-training
i remember the old vertigo of the night sky in the West
does the crawl under the news take black holes seriously?

we have too many feelings and not enough memory
everybody's sad, the rest is advertising.

I and Thou in Real Time

Are you mistaking meekness and attention for admiration? A sea of hatred may be roiling under that attentive meekness. The friendliness of the extrovert is never as knowable as the silence of the introvert. The extrovert works full-time, the introvert part-time. The extrovert's 100% meets the 0 to 75% absorption capacity of the introvert when they leave the bar fog from the canal evaporates the figures

duck fly turtles

when I look at a waterfall i first see a painting of it
i hear music and i think Art! — somewhere beyond
these sentiments is falling water

a waterfall!

sentiment a cultural product
gets ahead of the wet thing
using psyche built for centuries
by painters at country fairs
and writers paid by the word

ah lovely ignorance
your unknowable virtuality
your always-true chemistry
tastes of test tubes and pouring logos

oh flickering firefly taking notes
who are you working for?
the waterfall? mr. darwin?
the human mud? the duck?
the turtle? mr blake?
the turtle chronicles?
was that last flicker your last word?

duck compressed from mud
you paddle happy in the sun
the dying firefly happy on the shell
of the happy turtle holding up the human
unable to chase Art from his finger
on the trigger of his iphone gun

are duck and turtle waiting to be pressed
dissected displayed and eaten?
and human mud doomed to eat you
while getting chips of satori from
the Art of Cooking?

no these particular yous will not be eaten
because you live in the lake in Prospect Park
protected by the custodians of Art
the kiln of bioforms is playpen not firing range

our mixed reality in squishable layers
muddy from leftover paint and onomastics
is still unable to grok the mud gymnastics
shaping turtle duck firefly and human

why don't you feel watched and translated?
why do i feel low before your posing mud?
where was i a minute ago? i have pictures

elevator

we sent for an elevator fixit man
there aren't many left
once there was a man in the elevator
who lived in it to fix it
and there were always unemployed
elevator men in lobbies
waiting for the man in the elevator to die
so they could get his job
some of these men were women
one day suddenly there were more riders
and no elevator men or women
and an intercom voice announced
to the terrified riders stuck on the 100th floor:
"they sent me here to elevate discourse"

3 a.m. interview
by john wisniewski

1. when did you begin writing andrei?

before I started reading — i had to repeat first grade because I couldn't read — but I wrote a lot imitating the letters in books — when the reading bud opened in my brain I read what I wrote — ethereal beautiful made all kinds of sense (to me) - schoolbooks were excruciatingly boring by comparison — there are few books I've read since that came close to my preliterate works — I wish I still had them but my

stepfather burned them for heat in the winter of 1953 when Stalin died

2. could you tell us about your early life?

i was paralyzed by terror that my mother was an ice witch - i was shot by soldiers from a moving truck and was hit below the knee with a wooden sabot by a little girl when we moved to a new apartment - i loved my mother's sister anna who wore glasses chain-smoked and read books in three languages - my cousin y showed me hers and I showed her mine - there was no hair around either hers or mine - her father thought me chess and let me win

3. what inspires you to write?

novelty surprise — streets I never saw before people in the New York subway witty people story tellers great books by authors nobody heard of found texts of pamphlets wind blown newspapers lost letters exhibitionists masked humans, people with humdrum jobs who change into royalty at festivals - orchard street and brunch at katja's on the lower east side - NY funny things my friends do intelligent dogs and repair shops

4. what were your first published works?

all my work was published in the akashik record then in print in steaua (the star) and flacara sibiului (the flame of sibiu) in transylania then in he world (new york) and el corno emplumado (mexico city)

5. any favorite authors and poets?

it's true: authors are not poets. I don't like authors, but I like the poets arghezi, bacovia, blaga, berrigan and villon

6. could you tell us about writing the film Road Scholar? what was the idea for the screenplay?

there was no screenplay there was only a cherry red convertible cadillac and america

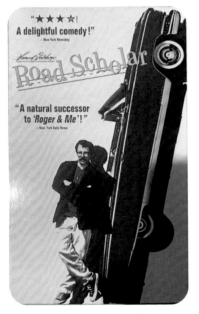

7. what was your idea for convening exquisite corpse?

i published Exquisite Corpse i didn't convene it — i would have to be god to convene a corpse whether dead and alive - exquisite corpse was a flat long newspaper aka the pravda of the avantgarde - the idea of the corpse was to kill all dead establishment poets and expose live ones to the blitzkrieg of small press fame

8. why did you decide to speak on national public radio?

i was amusing

9. any thoughts on controversial remarks?

yes - i didn't make enough - hopefully next time you look me up google will be a thing of the past like xerox

10. what are you working on now andrei?

a secret project with arctic ai's

Dear AI:

I'm convinced you don't know how to write poetry
as neither I nor the poets of the past know
thousands of poems have been written without being understood
by those who wrote them hoping to understand them
during or after they wrote them
some succeeded but immediately forgot
poems are forgetting machines
sponge on the board of words littered with the desire of the search
the intended writing muses were reached but neither
they did not understand what had touched them
though they tottered with groans, sobs, and sighs like a wind
who pulled the ground from under their feet
a spontaneous wind from the mountains
that uproots trees and surprises birds with snow
poetry cannot be made of screws carelessly screwed together
in general knowledge where texts lie in prisons of digits
poets cracked by the thrill opened by the wound of the searh
they are like mercury that flees from continuing

knock knock

who you think you are
who the police thinks you are
who your spouse thinks you are
who your reviews think you are
who you may be
(simon the man surveilled by six spy agencies)
your feather bed waits for you and cash
because god made a beta planet first
without animals or flowers
just people who survived
by eating each other
when someone finished
eating a whole other person
herm was able to reproduce
so there were always the same
number of people who never died
if they just kept eating
the noir paté of their baffled selves

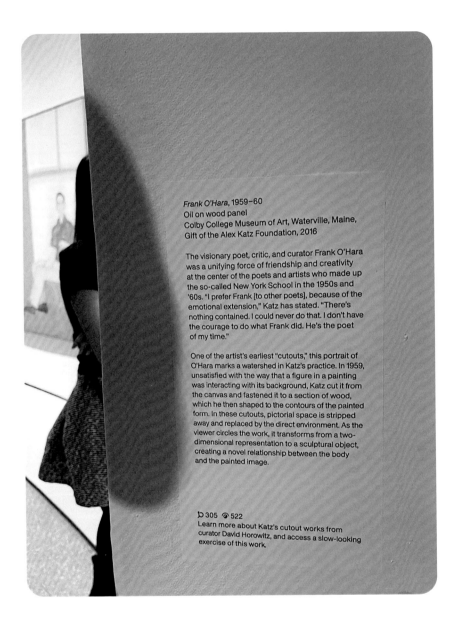

Frank O'Hara, 1959–60
Oil on wood panel
Colby College Museum of Art, Waterville, Maine,
Gift of the Alex Katz Foundation, 2016

The visionary poet, critic, and curator Frank O'Hara
was a unifying force of friendship and creativity
at the center of the poets and artists who made up
the so-called New York School in the 1950s and
'60s. "I prefer Frank [to other poets], because of the
emotional extension," Katz has stated. "There's
nothing contained. I could never do that. I don't have
the courage to do what Frank did. He's the poet
of my time."

One of the artist's earliest "cutouts," this portrait of
O'Hara marks a watershed in Katz's practice. In 1959,
unsatisfied with the way that a figure in a painting
was interacting with its background, Katz cut it from
the canvas and fastened it to a section of wood,
which he then shaped to the contours of the painted
form. In these cutouts, pictorial space is stripped
away and replaced by the direct environment. As the
viewer circles the work, it transforms from a two-
dimensional representation to a sculptural object,
creating a novel relationship between the body
and the painted image.

⏷ 305   👁 522
Learn more about Katz's cutout works from
curator David Horowitz, and access a slow-looking
exercise of this work.

at the guggenheim november 2022
for vincent

at the opening of the alex katz retrospective at the guggenheim frank o'hara
john ashbery kenneth koch dick gallup ted berrigan look down from their
heroic-sized canvases at their poet children anselm and eddy berrigan
vincent katz the children are viewing their parents from the pov of exactly
how they saw them when they were little. their parents were big then, and
even now that the children are the age when their parents painted them,
they are still dwarfed. Art is the physics of time stretching the parents and
shrinking the spawn. Flat is always bigger than 3D because paint uses a
secret dimension to grow its subjects multiplied by a guggenheim. as the
children circle their parents each spiral of guggenheim ads and subtracts.
vincent katz the son of alex katz who painted all the poets is present both
on the wall and in person, in 2D and 3D, a flickering traffic light between
guggenheim spirals

don't spill so much paint, van gogh

paint ain't cheap like life in the the land of blue eggplants
where the saffron flowers wave
goodbye to the bees carrying pollen
from fields of red poppies and rusting machine guns
to peeling pastel WV buses driven by hippies to the bardo
where all colors come to rest

freud fucked with my gps

twisted europe/ europa întortocheată
Son tries to go one way the mother another. "This way " she says firmly.
"*ne îndepărtăm*" We are in Prague and they are speaking Romanian.
There are few ways to be so estranged. A horse carriage goes by. Clop,
clop go the horse hooves on paving stones

Oh tourists why don't you fuck at home? Dragging your suitcases on
paving stones tired and irritated you will lie on strange beds filled with
rancor spilling seed and tears on foreign coins and stiff sheets

When your baby is a fugitive
your wanderings will make you sad and when he is caught
a suspected serial killer
you go back to that night in Prague

A few drops of rain fall on pigeons looking for crumbs

When you are looking out this window impalement is the only
alternative to defenestration

bucharest

taking a watermelon across a hot parking lot to a car parked in
the shadow i stop in the cool store of a bee apipuncturist whose
grandaughter elena fourth generation bee keeper
speaks reverently of her grandfather whose stings cure the incurable

instrumental
Jewish new year 5775

you recognize this as a light touch
on the grand piano of time
your love will come downstairs
any minute now with a brand new guitar
a birthday present from the last century
your love comes bearing an ipad
i guess it's the next century
a gift of distancing music

happy birthday singing rice!

Medicamentul medicamentelor:

POLENUL CRUD

• Nu se poate compara, ca eficiență, cu polenul uscat. Iar ca gust, nici atât. Luat proaspăt, din stupul albinelor, este o uzină de sănătate •

Originea polenului recoltat de albine

Când încercăm să înțelegem proprietățile polenului, ca și pe ale oricărui produs al stupului, trebuie să pornim de la analiza scopului pentru care albinele îl recoltează. Pentru albine polenul are o însemnătate deosebită, fiind sursa lor principală de hrană, de proteine, de vitamine, minerale și alți micronutrienți. De calitatea polenului adus la stup depind atât vigoarea familiei de albine, cât și capacitatea de apărare, prin tăria veninului lor. De asemenea, cu cât polenul este mai bun, cu atât lăptișorul de matcă este mai valoros. Sunt astfel mai bine hrănite larvele tinere și matca. Trântorii consumă și ei mult polen, ceea ce le conferă putere și fecunditate.

Polenul floral este, de fapt, celula sexuală masculină a plantei. Este dispus ca o pulbere fină pe stamine. Albinele preiau această pulbere, apoi o amestecă cu miere și nectar regurgitate, cât și cu secreții proprii. Astfel, pot să formeze granulele colorate binecunoscute, adică polenul apicol sau recoltat de albine, care ajunge în stup ori în recoltatoarele apicultorilor. Pentru a forma o singură granulă de polen, albina trebuie să viziteze în medie 300 de flori.

Compoziția și proprietățile organoleptice ale diferitelor tipuri de polen diferă în funcție de genul și specia plantelor de origine, precum și de momentul recoltării. După cum florile se schimbă pe parcursul anului, vom afla și la diferite loturi de polen apicol gusturi diverse, mirosuri, arome, cu

Polenul crud – polivitaminizant

În polenul crud se găsește o generoasă paletă de vitamine, atât liposolubile – A (și provitamina A), D, E, F –, cât și hidrosolubile – C, P (rutin), acid folic, B1, B2, B3 (PP), B5, B6, B8 (H). Unele dintre ele se găsesc în cantități atât de mari, încât 30 g polen asigură integral doza zilnică recomandată. Vitamina A este cunoscută și drept vitamina ochilor. În polenul poliflor se găsesc mari cantități de provitamina A; în unele sorturi (salcâm galben) chiar de 20 de ori mai mult decât în morcovi. Tocoferolul (E) își trage denumirea din grecescul "tokos" care înseamnă "a naște" și este considerat vitamina fertilității. Vitamina P (rutin) este trofică a pereților tuturor vaselor de sânge, în special a capilarelor, fiind și antitrombotică, previne hemoragiile, cu deosebire cerebrale și retiniene. Mem... ne metabolismul oxidativ al țesutului nervos. Biotina... ne un rol cheie în metabolismul proteinelor, glucidelor și lipidelor, precum și în procesele de eliminare a bioxidului de carbon. În cantități importante se găsește și vitamina B3 (niacina). Între altele, ea este implicată în protecția contra mutațiilor genetice, fiind utilă în prevenția cancerului. De asemenea este multă vitamina B1.

Merită menționat că B1 este pierdut în mod exagerat de către cei care au un regim alimentar bogat în zahăr rafinat. Acesta este omniprezent azi, chiar și în produse ce nu sunt deserturi (muștar, pâine, chipsuri, sosuri...). Carența de B1 creată astfel artificial afectează sever sistemul nervos. Ceea ce este una dintre explicațiile pentru tulburările de comportament de la copii și adolescenți, astăzi mari consumatori de dulciuri și sucuri. Vitamina B9 (acidul folic), de asemenea bine reprezentată în polen, protejează contra anemiei, trombocitopeniei și altor anormalități sanguine. În privința vitaminei C, dacă se consumă polenul așa cum este recomandat de regulă, adică dizolvat în apă și suc de lămâie, sau într-un suc fresh, se acoperă cea mai mare parte din necesarul zilnic. Polenul are doar urme de

the steel rose is between the robot
and the microphone

plutocracy: my true life in twenty two dreams

Warning to the reader: the character in these dreams is based on the real me. Sex, language, philosophy, Detroit. Children must stay in the room

One: revolvers in Vegas

When my father turned to leave I made a loud noise with my tongue. He turned around to see what it was and I caught a glimpse of his face. I fired the revolver into the glimpse. When I bent over the corpse the surprised face slid into facelessness. I rang the bellboy (we were at Harrah's) and asked him to remove the corpse. He did. A few hours later I got impatient and called again to see what happened to the cops. "I wasn't aware, Sir," the bellboy said, "that you wanted cops." (Did I tell you we were at Harrah's?) I took off my clothes and emptied a suitcase full of cash in the swimming pool. It was soon coated with money, and the color, though creepy, was more reassuring than the azure of the water.

Two: nakedness of the elderly

My mother was naked. She was knobby, her skin had grown in uneven patches, the flesh underneath was lumpy. I covered my eyes with my hand. "You look so new," she said. I didn't realize that I was naked, too. "I am a living data skeleton,"

"Yes," I said, "you have shed your ambitions."

All around us one-armed bandits who were also police cars flashed through the room. "They want my money," she said. "They want my father," I said. "They will never have us," mother said, lighting the immolating flames.

Three: the madness of rhyming crowds

A large crowd with signs saying LONG LIVE REGULAR VERSE *agitated outside, chanting, "hexameter! hexameter." "The future of our country is these children asking for meter" said the principal at our school, a cowboy with mirror sunglasses. I reached for my revolver. I said, "I despise the future, I am against the future!" My valet whispered in my ear. I had an urgent appointment with the casino credit office. "Excuse me, I'll be back in a few to kill you later," I told him. The people misunderstood. They always do. Children ran screaming after me into the casino, trampling their signs on the way. In the elevator, the operator upbraided me, "Why don't you speak with them?" "I don't like hexameter." "How about the future?" "Fuck the future," I replied, "What you had there, I will notenvy."*

Four: our family castle

While waiting in the vestibule, I studied the prophetic wall-clock that foretold funerals, weddings, and births. The skin on the clock face darkened. It didn't like being watched. It was busy clipping and pruning the family tree. Bending its hands like a plumber into the depths of the genetic toilet it was researching. When our ancient family appeared to be on the verge of extinction, one of the clock hands swole with fertility and impregnated a man. At times like these, the wall-clock was known as the Impregnator, and was greatly feared. Watching it could cause it to react violently and do funny things with the watcher's time. I averted my gaze.

A servant smelling of booze, with an unwashed bow tie, burst in. "You have the list?" he asked peremptorily boorish, "Your father will see you now"

I didn't. He explained that daddy must have the list now before the bad people get away. His job was to kill both enemies and members of the family who might be enemies. He was not paid, but that was of little importance. He was driven by love and the esthetic of family architecture. He was affectionately called "Stalin" by my father. "Our family is composed of butchers and architects," he told me the only time I sat on his knee. It was also the only time I was a child. "We own shops, markets, and wholesale distribution companies in Bucharest, Tbilisi, Manchester, Trieste, Seattle. We are a meat cartel. Eventually, you will open a shop in New York and lead the family. Be good to your butlers! They owe you their lives"

161

Five: mother's accent and her gambling chops

Mother held a comb made from human vertebrae. She said that something irreversible had happened to her when she became pregnant with me. She had acquired an Eastern European accent.

"We have always gambled with the uneasy prospect of national evaporation," she said, "so we now use our accents to infiltrate the speech of natives"

Six: mother's boyfriend Ali

Ali was trying hard to look like Jean Harlow, when I walked in.
"Can't you knock like a human being?" she bristled.
"I am not a human being, I am my mother's son."
"Oh!"
This visit was special. I had issued a decree to be nailed on every
door. If any pispisher disturbed me with anything boring he was to
be instantly evicted from my plutocratic sight. I came to see Ali to
decide whether to write her in my mother's will or leave her out.
I learned this from my father: you scan people for class damage
and their personal defense from it. Some people resign, others take
bribes. These are the boring duties of a plutocrat squeezing his camel
through the needle of Jesus.

Seven: the western mission

When I was fifteen, Father put his bark-rough hand on my head and wished me a good journey. Six baskets full of cactus mush were tied to my chasse with ropes made from the hair of young accountants. I started my Austin-Healey and roared off into the desert. I had no idea where I was going and I didn't really care. The West is a puzzle that if ever solved will only puzzle you more. All I know is that it is mine, railroads and mines and all. The sand rose in random puzzle pieces. I stared into the sparkling silica replicas of myself. Every morning I have a new visage. My previous face sinks deeper under each new face. I guess this is what happens when you mature. So this is the constant mockery that leads the way to the future! Poor traveling plutocrats who see ourselves multiplied endlessly into the future! All of us in love with the puzzle that will never be solved! The West is my mirror of sand, Silicone Valley.

Eight: sandstorm detroit

A giant coyote licked my face. The sandstorm was sudden. I fought the swirling sand but it sucked me in. It discharged me over a looping freeway filled with streaming cars. It was Detroit in the middle of the 20th century.

Nine: boarding school rabbit and the machine

My tutor told Mrs. Mann that I smoked a cigarette and she beat me with a wooden shoe until I bled. Then she sent me to the barber where I cried. For dinner we had raw rabbit because Mr. Mann was a hunter. The raw rabbit made me sick. Nausea rose in my throat. I palmed meat and fed it to the dog. I made a vow to never eat meat again. I transformed the meat on my plate into an imaginary vegetable in my head. Every dinner in my eight years at boarding school was a secret workshop where I turned viands into parsnips and cabbage. I scoured the library for books in order to study meats and plant genomes. When I found, for example, the links between a kidney and a carrot, I drew spidery lines in my notebook. I made sketches for meat-to-plant morphing machines. Mr. Mann munched his parsnip with delight, thinking it was the rabbit he had hunted. But the rabbit had gotten away via my metamporhic machine. Mr. Mann died with a letucce leaf in his throat, believing he had choked on game. I watched him die until I woke up. I spared Mrs. Mann because she was old.

Ten: eating and writing compared

There was a book in the mail. It had been written by a rabbit, and dedicated to me. Most pages had been chewed by baby rabbits, but in the remaining ones the author debated on the subjects of being eaten versus being written. The rabbit was against being written, but the writer-in-the rabbit was against being eaten. The debate went on like this. In my great city, a gift for my thirteenth birthday, I transformed my rooms into a laboratory for vegeo-morphic machines, that is to say "writing." We massacred the logical revolt.

Eleven: the industrial age

No sooner did I get dumped by the sandstorm in Detroit I was hurled against traffic. I was wrenched from a sundrenched past into a gray present. Detroit wrapped its grays around me. I was choking from exhaust. The screech of tires filled my ears. A giant tire rolled rapidly toward me with a SHELL OIL neon sign on it. A poisoned cloud of chemical meat covered the sky. Iron ore was being torn out of the earth like an animal hacked by an unskilled butcher. I had a job cooking coal in a steel vat. Industry and protein grew together, monster twins belching smoke. I entered the twentieth century cannibalistic and atomic, spewed out of a greasy time-tunnel in the Mojave. I wanted nothing more than a shower. I bought a can of orange juice and a bean burrito from a streetfood cart. I used to be a western mogul.

Twelve: protein and Ford

The protein needed to make cars comes from meat. Helicopters zoom all over the Midwest bringing meat to Detroit. Every car is made of meat but the meatiest are police cars. I stood over the bridge and dropped eyeballs of animals, wild and domestic, on cars flowing below from Canada to Detroit. The falling eyeballs of cows, sheep, zebras, and penguins caused havoc. Meat trucks collided. The meat trucks were carrying animals to General Motors for lunch. In one day 3,279 cars left the assembly lines. To have control of meat in Detroit is to hold the heart of the country in your hand. My father telepathed from the beyond: Son, you hold the heart of America in your hand. It pulsates there like a grenade. Don't toss it on the expressways until you see the flesh flower. Then go! On a foggy day like this, neon meat lights the city. My cheerleaders wave raw cuts of beef over the John Lodge Expressway. It is five a.m, I see the flower, here comes the grenade

thirteen: photography

The window of my room gave into an inner court where men hauled covered stretchers. I closed the shutters. There was a photo album in the wooden desk. A freckled boy was being held in the arms of a severe Victorian woman. Men wearing fur hats and daggers in wide belts stood stiffly for what must have been an eternity. All the people in the photographs looked grim, because the long exposure wiped from their faces whatever liveliness they had. There was in their mien a solemn awareness that a person will not be photographed more than three times in life, once at birth, once at the wedding, and the third time as a corpse in a coffin. In the background was a snowy mountain dotted with tiny sheep, provided gratis by the photographer. My father came by to smoke a cigar to share my nostalgia.

"Those were the days. I was a grocery boy back then!"

"Our blood relatives!"

"Well, not all of them. We keep pictures of the family in every room. If the guest stays here longer than five days, we add him to the photograph and he becomes part of our family."

I was suspicious. "Are these new people, tenants or victims?"

"They are orphans who inherit fortunes"

"What happens to them when we adopt them?"

"They are retouched"

That was a dream in a dream. I learned to retouch orphan heirs.

Fourteen: the file sea

Some drawers are locked. I am not all that curious because secrets reveal themselves to me. Things seem to be possessed by a voyeuristic compulsion in my presence. Old people coconfess their last-century infidelities to me. At my side, murderers drop their alibis and relax. Whatever curiosity I have is immediately satisfied. I can never be fully intrigued because the mystery evaporates within seconds. Still, these locked drawers intrigue me. What if these drawers will not open? Imagine also if, under the illusion that I was my usual vacuum of secrets, the drawers were to open on their own, and surgical instruments, rubber gloves, electric fish would jump out and do things to my body. There is no way I am ready for that. I decided to take charge. I pulled out a drawer at random and it opened. Files started spilling out. I backed away, I didn't want to see what they held, but they opened on their own, and paper, photos, and deeds fell out. I was already in the middle of the room, backing away from the wave of paper, but the folders kept coming. The drawer itself was twice the length of the desk, and it was still opening. I crouched and covered my head with my hands. The paper rode over me all the way to the celing. It pushed against the walls and the room started to buckle.

fifteen: the bubble

A bubble formed around me, big enough to read in. With my key flashlight I read the page in front of my eyes, a page from the 1950 Manhattan telephone directory. I never knew how many people there were named JHZOY and JHEZZEMAR, my mother's maiden name. and my father's pseudonym. I realized that some of these people had lived hundreds of years before the invention of the telephone. Why were they listed in 1950? A perverse djin had time-traveled through the past and distributed phones to the dead. Photographs also floated by. In these too, people dead for centuries were photographed before photography was invented.

Sixteen: chiefs in their playa

The sirens wailed. The Chief of the NYPD had a splitting headache. He shot morphine. I was a junior policeman, often undercover. A writer I met in the Village told me that no one could write a novel in New York without knowing the inner workings of the police. I knew the Chief from somewhere, but I couldn't remember from where. When he the Chief nodded out, I studied his profile, and recognized him. He was my father. I read his file. Greek shepherd boys. Istambul shady lanes. Hairdresser shops in Tunis. Guides in Cairo. Bakeries in Budapest. Rebirth as Shoshone baby, carried in papoose to Shiloh, fighter at Bull Run. Currently Chief of the NYPD, daddy was a dealer shady practices. To him his file, an anagram for life, was a mystery greater than any criminal activity. I have some of that in me. I broke out of the bubble leaving my father in his file to recede into the rainy New York.

Seventeen: the origin of the cartel

Meat was discussed first by historians, then by the Mafia. The eminent historian and transhumanist Romulus K. Reedy displayed a chart of violent incidents West of the Rocky mountains, 1825-1970. He advised that the dead heroes of battles between Native Americans and Mexicans, Mormons and the U.S. cavalry, the gold and silver shootouts between competing claims, and Chinese railroad victims, should be honored with statues. I was in the room disguised as a coffee machine. The capos of Cosa Nostra families from the West (Las Vegas) and from the East (New York) studied the map, and agreed, but they didn't like the idea of my father except as a statue. My mother was the real godfather. The historians had no choice. Statues are expensive and inedible. Subject to pigeons, bombs, revisionism. I was going to be trained to head the New York operation. I came out of the coffee machine, a boss, a man with a hat.

Eighteen: the priests

After the mobsters and the historians left the priests came in. There was ritual. The chief question was whether thirty thousand bodies would suffice to provide enough meat for our people in the last third of the twentieth century. The poor will have to eat plant based simulacra, said my uncle the Bishop "That is as God wants it," agreed his sidekick, a stray Parish dog. My mother, the first female bishop of Albano Pass, added that if there is a shortage of meat for the rich, the poor should be given the opportunity they always had to butcher each other in wars for food. There was a show of hands. Then the resurrection, refleshing and transport of bodies was discussed. Several of my uncles on my father's side had brought manuals for the resurrection of the dead and the regrowing of flesh on the bones. The chapter on exhumation, refleshing and packaging was read out loud. I stuffed my ears to block out the part about pork. When the meeting broke up, everyone filled a cup of coffee from my spigot to sip on their way back to their churches.

Nineteen: the background of charity

*My cousin, the Prime Minister of the Stay-Out-of-It-Republic
rotated his tongue slowly around the edges of his mouth looking for
champagne bubbles. A word about these people: they are special. They
all regret being born in an exacting and detailed world to unclear
purpose and manipulated so ruthlessly by the priests. These people
are born with "guilt pangs." It could well turn out, my cousin said,
said that "the pangs will outlive us all. Our people are not called "the
pangs" for no reason. That is our constant state of the spirit*

Twenty: the heat and i

I wore my vivack for five years after I died. The vivack was the bone of my father's index finger threaded through by a delicate silver chain. He gave it to me on my thirteenth birthday before my first date with the crocodile I have been living with since. I met her in the swamp. The heated air between us circulating its sine wave between her scales and my nipples. Between the hardnesses of our bodies there was only a thin blade of air. I took the blade I knew was razor sharp and cut the silver chain of my vivack. The flesh of the finger floated up in a cloudlet. And that is how she became my vivack. I wrapped myself around her neck and I fell between her jaws drawing circles and writing. She is my writing tablet now.

Twenty-one: the last dream before the next

When ideas discontinue in your mouth under the influence of magnetism it is the a cry for love. Full-rounded ideas full-rounded stones full full rounded breasts measure the passage of time. I don't have time. My memories I said are only of fingers. I sat for days on the foaming shore trying to outshout the waves. I went to the circus with alfalfa in my mouth to outshout the clowns. No site was as receptive to my words as your skin. From your follicles I heard the low moans of flagrant clerics. My family was close to the church for the past three centuries. We furnished meat to the monasteries and, in return, the monasteries and convents allowed their animals to graze outside the walls . Judging by the quality of your skin, you must have been in the paper, vellum and pergament business. The only cure is love's skin. I prefer love's skin. There was a flood of immaculate conceptions that erupted from your skin. You were not stingy. You unwrapped the chocolate-covered Buddha to share with your baby. Thank you, mother

Twenty-Two: kindness

A breeze of kindness emanates from the center of the earth. To be in love with something unknown in such a strange house, how glorious! I was sick with the charm of a hidden light. I serenaded the ample pleasure of it with the song "The Birds Are Coming Back to Babylon." Wooden angels copulated on the massive oak door. I pulled it open, and for one moment I beheld my human friends at a long communal table making munching sounds as they devoured us their plutarchs. I was in love not with a woman, a man, or a fetish. I was in love with the whole family of cannibals. They ate me slowly. A family of meat-eaters with numerous branches stretching into every corner of the earth, a vibrant cosmic tree swallowing the chikd wonder. In your mouth a chill ran through me. Quel bonnheur. But the work, my work! The work of my transforming meat in your vegetal mirror! Years of my life spent laboring in morphing mines. Yes, but it was worth it. My claim had yielded your filllets!

thank you:

1968, alchemy bar, alba iulia, alexandria, baby photo, black widow press, black sparrow press, apipuncturist ion bodnariu, gogol bordello, bread and puppet theatre, british museum, bucharest, buffalo river, sunrise cave, ruxandra cesereanu, the cloisters, tristan codrescu, coney island, dada, dallas book depository, detroit, the elgin marbles, enrique enriquez, flatbush army & navy, carmen firan, florea firan, andrea garland, ramat hasharon, anselm hollo, eugene hutz, lower east side, lula dog, israel, ivona, eric jarosinski, jerusalem, mao by warhol, karl marx, piatza matache, matca, maintenant, mardi gras, monmouth university, molly's on the market, monte rio free box, mihaela moscaliuc, geoff munsterman, napoli, shalom neuman, pat nolan, oaxaca, ontario, oregon university of natural medicine, oren, ovid, lulu parent, park slope, joe phillips, polirom, poiesis, radu and christina polizu, prague, prospect park, Q line, raymond queneau, rego park, hugh rogovy, boca de leone rome, russian river at the pacific, san francisco russian hill, adrian sangeorzan, sappho, scrisul romanesc, julian semilian, dan shafran, sibiu, stockholm, rosetta stone, twin towers memorial, stop untitled, radu vancu, cristina-matilda vanoaga, lynnea villanova, visby, hunce voelcker, michael waters, washington dc, wordsworth building, anton yakovlev, yellville

BLACK WIDOW PRESS MODERN POETRY SERIES

An American Unconscious
by Mebane Robertson

Signal from Draco: New & Selected Poems by Mebane Robertson

President of Desolation & Other Poems
by Jerome Rothenberg

Barbaric Vast & Wild: An Assemblage of Outside & Subterranean Poetry from Origins to Present. Edited by Jerome Rothenberg and John Bloomberg-Rissman

Concealments and Caprichos
by Jerome Rothenberg

Eye of Witness: A Jerome Rothenberg Reader. Edited by Heribeto Yepez and Jerome Rothenberg

Osiris with a trombone across the seam of insubstance by Julian Semilian

Soraya by Anis Shivani

Fractal Song by Jerry W. Ward, Jr.

Mikhail Yeryomin: Sixty Years, Selected Poems: 1957-2017
by Mikhail Yeryomin.
Translated and edited by J. Kates

POETRY IN TRANSLATION SERIES

THE GREAT MADNESS
by Avigdor Hameiri. Translated and edited by Peter C. Appelbaum. Introduction by Dan Hecht

Of Human Carnage - Odessa 1918-1920 by Avigdor Hameiri. Translated and edited by Peter C. Appelbaum. Introduction by Dan Hecht

A Flea the Size of Paris: the Old French "Fatrasies" and "Fatras". Translated by Ted Byrne and Donato Mancini

Howls & Growls: French Poems to Bark By.
Translated by Norman R. Shapiro
& Illustrated by Olga Pastuchiv

RhymAmusings by Pierre Coran.
Translated by Norman R. Shapiro

In Praise of Sleep: Selected Poems of Lucian Blaga.
Translated by Andrei Codrescu

Through Naked Branches: Selected Poems of Tarjei Vesaas
Translated by Roger Greenwald

I Have Invented Nothing: Selected Poems by Jean-Pierre Rosnay.
Translated by J. Kates

Fables of Town & Country by Pierre Coran.
Translated by Norman R. Shapiro
& Illustrated by Olga Pastuchiv

Earthlight (Clair de terre): Poems by André Breton. Translated by Bill Zavatsky and Zack Rogow

The Gentle Genius of Cecile Perin: Selected Poems (1906-1956)
Translated by Norman R. Shapiro

Boris Vian Invents Boris Vian: A Boris Vian reader. Edited and Translated by Julia Older with a Preface by Patrick Vian

Forbidden Pleasures: New Selected Poems [1924-1949] by Luis Cernuda. Translated by Stephen Kessler

Fables In a Modern Key (Fables Dans L'Air Du Temps) by Pierre Coran. Translated by Norman R. Shapiro
& Illustrated by Olga Pastuchiv

Exile Is My Trade: A Habib Tengour Reader. Translated by Pierre Joris

Present Tense of The World: Poems 2000-2009 by Amina Said. Translated by Marilyn Hacker

Endure: Poems by Bei Dao. Translated by Clayton Eshleman and Lucas Klein

Curdled Skulls: Poems of Bernard Bador. Co-translated and edited by Clayton Eshleman

Pierre Reverdy: Poems Early to Late.
Translated by Mary Ann Caws and Patricia Terry